The Woman

in the

Mirror

Rashanda Minnis

Dedication

To my son, Rashawn Minnis—

You are the reason I kept going when life tried to break me.

You are my greatest accomplishment, my deepest love, and my constant motivation.

May you always walk with pride, purpose, and peace— knowing that your mother overcame every storm to give you a better life.

This book is for you.

And to every woman who was ever counted out—

May you find your voice, your strength, and your crown in these pages.

You are not alone. You are not broken. You are becoming.

Acknowledgement

To God
Thank you for never leaving me, even when I doubted,
even when I was lost. Your grace covered me in my darkest
moments and lifted me when no one else could. You are my
constant, my strength, and my peace.

To my siblings
Even in the distance, even through the misunderstandings,
you are still my blood. We all fought our own battles in our
own ways. I love you regardless.

To my father
You were my calm in the chaos. The one who saw me when
I felt invisible. Thank you for your presence and your
steady heart.

To every person who doubted me
Your words became the fire beneath my wings. I thank you
because I turned your doubt into drive.

To my supporters
Whether you followed my businesses, encouraged me
silently, or stood by me through hard times—I see you. I
thank you.

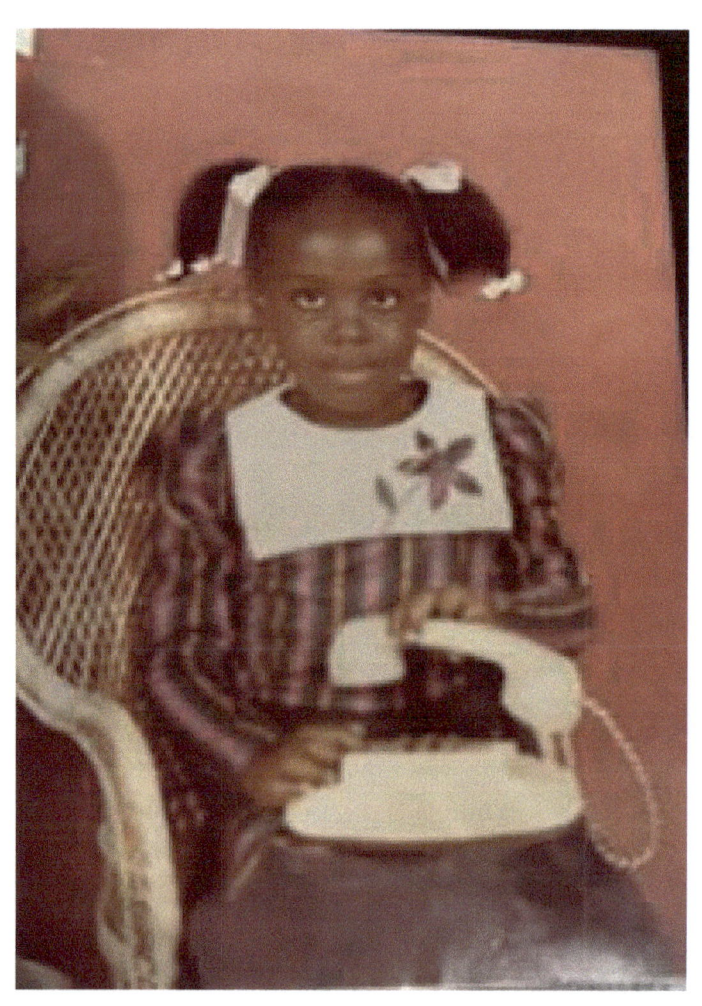

Table of Contents

Chapter 1
The Beginning

I was born on October 5, 1979, in Nassau, Bahamas. I am the youngest of five children. I had three older sisters and one brother. Since my brother lived with our grandparents, so I grew up mostly surrounded by my sisters and often, I felt like an outsider. The age gap between me and the next closest sibling was ten years, which meant I was practically raised alone.

My childhood was challenging and far from joyful. I felt unloved and unwanted by my mother, whose affection seemed reserved for everyone else but me. I never understood why I was treated differently, but her coldness left a deep impact.

My only comfort was my father. I was his baby, and he made me feel like I mattered. In a home that often made me feel invisible, he was the light I clung to. When people say children only need one person to believe in them, I understand what that means — because, for me, that person was my dad.

Despite having siblings, I often felt alone, like a shadow that nobody acknowledged. I was talked down to, overlooked, and labeled the black sheep. That label stuck with me for years. It hurt, especially when it came from my own family. They would say things like, "You'll never be anything," or "You won't amount to much." I heard those words so often that they became part of me. After a while, I even started to believe them. Most of those words came from my mother, the one who should be proud of me and support me.

I was a child craving love. A little girl just wanting someone, especially her mother, to say, "I'm proud of you." But those words never came. Still, I kept going. I had no choice.

Chapter 2
School Days

School became my outlet — my escape. I started at CW Sawyer, then transferred to Bahamas Academy. It was a more organized, private school, and while I didn't love it, I was familiar with the system. But one day, everything changed. My mother took me out of that private school and enrolled me in Government High School. I'll never forget how it felt — like being thrown into a different world.

I was furious. I didn't understand why she did it. I felt like it was a punishment, another reminder that I wasn't worth keeping in something good. That switch made me bitter, angry, resentful. And I acted out.

At Government High, I quickly gained popularity — but not for reasons most people would be proud of. I was rebellious, outspoken, and didn't care much for rules. I was known for pushing boundaries. But for me, it wasn't about seeking attention — it was about survival. It was my way of coping with the rejection I felt at home.

I joined everything I could — dance team, cheerleading, and Junior Junkanoo. Being part of those groups brought me joy. I could express myself in ways I couldn't at home. When I was dancing or performing, I didn't feel like the black sheep. I felt alive. I felt seen.

But my mother didn't approve of any of it. She frowned upon everything I did. To her, dancing was inappropriate, cheerleading was a distraction, and Junkanoo was a waste of time. She never celebrated my talents; instead, she criticized them. Eventually, she'd had enough of my so-called "disobedience" and kicked me out of the house.

She sent me to live with my older sister. My father — the one person I always felt safe with — thought it was the best decision at the time. That broke me. I felt like I was being thrown away again.

Even through the pain, I kept pushing. I also joined the school's softball team, which gave me something else to focus on. Sports helped keep me grounded, even when everything else in my life felt unstable. I found discipline in the game. I discovered a kind of strength I didn't know I had.

Looking back, I now see that those school days were shaping me, even through the hurt. I learned how to stand tall amid judgment. I learned how to hold on to joy, even when it wasn't handed to me. And most importantly, I realized that I didn't need anyone's permission to be myself. I was young, wild, and free..

Chapter 3
Teenage Dreams

By my late teens, I had already experienced more than most girls my age. I was no stranger to hardship, rejection, and survival firsthand. I was living with my sister, but after discovering I was pregnant, she felt some kind of way, and still figuring out where I belonged in this world, I was back to square one. I longed for love, stability, and for someone to choose me for once.

At the tender age of 19, I became a mother, living in our abandoned house that my mother was trying to sell, with no light and no water, relying on neighbors. Having my son, Rashawn, changed everything. I was still just a girl myself, but the moment I looked into his eyes, I knew I had to grow up fast. I had to be the one to give him the love I always wanted. I was determined to break the cycle by being present, being nurturing, and being everything my own childhood lacked.

Being a teen mom wasn't easy. I worked nonstop up until I gave birth. I had no room for weakness. There was no maternity leave, no cozy baby showers, and no community to lean on. I thank God every day for his Grammy, his father's mom, my only help. I was working jobs in bars and restaurants, trying to survive and prepare for this new life I was bringing into the world.

I remember feeling exhausted emotionally, physically, and spiritually. But somehow, I kept going. I had no option. My son relied on me.

Those years were filled with dreams but also with pressure. I wanted more for myself, but I didn't know how to reach it. I thought maybe love could save me. Maybe if I just found someone to love me the right way, things would be okay.

That was the lie I held onto for years. That love — especially from a man — would heal all the wounds my family inflicted. But what I ended up finding were relationships that reflected the rejection I had always known.

I dreamed of a better life. I dreamed of being successful, having a home filled with peace, and raising my son with pride. I dreamed of being my own boss — and even though I didn't know how I'd get there, the dream never faded.

Even during my teenage years, with a baby on my hip and pain in my heart, I knew one thing: I was not going to stay down forever.

Chapter 4
A Roller Coaster Called Love

Love. That word followed me like a shadow my whole life. I chased it. Longed for it. Expected it to show up in the form of a man who would finally make me feel seen, safe, and wanted. But what I got was far from that.

My relationships became a series of emotional rollercoasters — dizzying highs followed by soul-crushing lows. The love I thought I found always came with conditions, pain, manipulation, and control. I endured abusive relationships for way too long. At first, I told myself it would get better. That if I just loved harder, if I gave more, it would fix the cracks. But the more I gave, the more they took — and the less of me I had left.

It started gradually. The name-calling. The isolation. The disrespect. Then it escalated to control, jealousy, and eventually physical abuse. I was broken down and exhausted, beaten and mistreated, with no more energy left to fight. I felt confused and lost. Love should not feel like this, I kept telling myself. "What is love?" was a question I always asked but could never truly answer.

In one of those relationships, I turned to alcohol. I thought it would numb the pain, help me escape, and silence the voices in my head that told me I wasn't enough. And for a short time, it worked — or so I thought. But the problems never went away; they were just waiting for me the next morning. The alcohol didn't erase the pain; it paused it. And when it returned, it returned louder.

7

I began to settle. I stayed in meaningless and abusive relationships, mistaking routine for security. I convinced myself that being in a loveless relationship was better than being alone, because at least then, I wouldn't feel abandoned. But in truth, I was lonelier in those relationships than I ever was by myself.

There were nights I cried myself to sleep next to someone who didn't even notice my tears. I gave my heart to men who didn't even bother to protect it. I loved men who didn't love me back, at least not in a way that was healthy, honest, or kind.

My life became a cycle: meet someone, believe in them, get hurt, start over. I began to wonder if maybe love simply wasn't for me. Or worse — that I didn't deserve it.

But deep down, I never stopped hoping. Because no matter how battered my heart became, it still beat with the belief that something better had to exist. That real love — the kind that heals and holds—was still out there even if I hadn't found it yet.

I moved to three different islands just to evade the possession of one of my relationships. You abused me, but did not want to live without me. How is this love? Why did I stay so long? Why would I let my child see this abuse?

My most meaningful relationship at the time came from a married man. I knew better and knew it was wrong, but it felt so right. He treated me the way I wanted to be treated, the way I knew love should be. How can I be so in love with someone that's not truly mine? Why would he take the time to learn me if he couldn't be with me? This was the fairytale

I dreamt about, the love I longed for. But after twenty-four years, I knew that somehow I had to walk away, as painful as it was, as distraught as I was. I know it's easy to mistake passion for purpose when your feelings lead the way, but emotions without evidence can lead to delusion.

The roller coaster of love taught me a hard truth: a man can never complete you, especially when you don't even know yourself. I was looking for someone to save me, when the saving had to start within. I began to realize that the love I was chasing in others could only be found in God and myself.

Chapter 5
Rising Again

There comes a moment when the pain no longer breaks you—it **builds you.**

After all the betrayals,heartbreaks, fights, and silence… I was still standing. Yes, I was bruised. Yes, I was tired. Yes, I've been hurt, but I was still here. And that meant I still had power.

The world had tried to count me out. Men had used me. The family had doubted me. Life had tossed me around like a rag doll. But I knew there was something **Greater inside me-** and I was ready to find her again.

It started with the small things.

I used to say "no" but now say "yes." I was praying when I wanted to give up. Smiling at my son and reminding myself that I was his **Whole World**. I had to **rebuild myself** from the inside out, not with money or validation, but with faith.

And it wasn't easy.

Healing doesn't come in a straight line. Some days I felt strong, and other days I wanted to crawl back into the pain just because it felt familiar. But slowly, day by day, I rose.

From the time I was a little girl, I knew I didn't want to work for anyone. I didn't have the language for it back then, but I knew I was built for something bigger.

The Woman in the Mirror

I spent years working in bars as a barmaid, waitress, hustling for tips, and working long nights. I saw all kinds of people and learn how to read a room fast. I knew when to smile, when to walk away, and how to handle myself in chaos. Those jobs taught me resilience, but they also reminded me that I wasn't meant to stay in that space forever. My last straw was when I worked for **the Italians.**

I started as a sales Rep, but it didn't take long before they promoted me to a manager. I was sharp, hard working, and got results, and they saw that. But what they didn't show was **appreciation.** I was doing more than what was required, running the show, and still being treated like I was disposable. That was my wake-up call. That's when I knew: **I will never give this much of myself to someone else's dream again.**

I also said one day I'll have something of my own, not just to make money but to create a life on my terms.

That day came

I opened my **boutique** first, a place where I could bring my style energy and personality into something tangible. Then came my **restaurant** business, a dream I poured my hands and heart into. Suddenly, I wasn't just working jobs, I was building Legacies.

And let me say this clearly:

Nobody handed me anything.

Nobody came and said, Here's your chance.

I created my chance.

I silenced the voices that said I wouldn't be anything, especially the ones that came from my own family. The ones who looked down on me laughed at me, expecting me to feel those voices lit a fire in me, and now they have no choice but to watch me shine.

Being my own boss isn't just about business, it's about **freedom**

Freedom to decide.

Freedom to protect my peace. Freedom to say, I built this and I did it while they said I couldn't.

I started dreaming again. I poured into my businesses. I surrounded myself with people who didn't just take from me, but people who spoke life into me. I started walking in my purpose, and not in my pain.

I had been through hell. But hell didn't have the last word- **God did**.

And his word said: "You are chosen. You are strong, you are not defined by what they did to you or what they think of you. You are stronger and wiser.

I had to rise not just for me, but for every woman who ever felt trapped, used, or thrown away. I had to rise for the girl in me who was told she'd never be anything. I had to rise because **my story was never meant to end in the valley.** It was meant to be told from the top of the mountain.

Chapter 6
The Woman in the Mirror

There was a moment when I looked in the mirror and didn't recognize the woman staring back at me.

Her eyes were weary and sunken. Her smile — if there was one — was forced. Her face told the story of someone who had endured too much for too long. She was once bold, full of spark and promise. Now, she just looked exhausted.

I had endured abuse, rejection, loneliness, and disappointment. I had poured my heart into relationships that drained me. I had lived for others, stayed in places where I was barely tolerated, and accepted love that often felt like punishment. And eventually, it all caught up with me.

That day, standing in front of the mirror, I asked myself: Who are you, Rashanda?

The truth hit hard — I had no idea. I had spent so many years trying to be what others needed, expected, or demanded that I had forgotten who I was. I was living on autopilot. Running businesses. Raising a son. Surviving. But I wasn't living. I wasn't free.

That was the moment something shifted in me.

I started seeing the woman in the mirror not as a failure or a victim, but as a fighter. A survivor. A queen who had been bent but never broken. I began to treat myself with the same grace I had given to so many others. I stopped settling. I stopped searching for worth in people who didn't value me.

13

I started to pray more. I started to heal. I started to believe — not because I was "saved" in some traditional way, but because I knew there had to be a higher power watching over me. The God who protected me when I was sleeping in a car, pregnant. The God who held me when nobody else would, the one who sent help when that guy tried to bury me alive. That same God had carried me this far, and I wasn't about to let go now.

Healing wasn't instant. Some days, the mirror still reflected pain. But gradually, I began to see a different reflection. One of strength, resilience, and a woman who had every reason to give up — but didn't. The woman in the mirror isn't perfect, but she's powerful. She's no longer seeking validation or trying to be chosen. She understands now that her worth isn't up for debate.

Now, when I look in the mirror, I see her.

Chapter 7
The Black Sheep's Crown

They always called me the black sheep.

Since I was little, I've been labeled, misunderstood, judged, and whispered about. I was the one who didn't quite fit in. The one who "talked back," who "acted out," and who "wasn't going to be anything." The one they said would fall flat, fail, and never rise. They didn't just say it behind closed doors — they said it to my face.

And for a while, I believed them. It hurts even more when it comes from your Mother. Why would the person who birthed you try to destroy you?

When you're constantly told you're not good enough, not smart enough, not worthy — it takes root. It grows inside you, wrapping itself around your confidence until you're left second-guessing your value. That was me. Always trying to prove myself. Always trying to be enough.

But over the years, something changed. With each trial I survived, each loss I endured, and every goal I quietly accomplished, I began to see the truth: **being the black sheep wasn't a curse — it was a crown.**

They underestimated me because they didn't know my strength. They dismissed me because they couldn't understand my calling. They tried to break me, but they ended up building me — unintentionally training me for the battles ahead.

Rashanda Minnis

The same girl they said wouldn't make it?

She became a business owner.
She raised a strong, respectful son.
She got up every time life tried to knock her down.
She didn't just survive — she *thrived.*

I didn't follow the path they expected. I didn't become what they approved of. But I became something greater — *myself.*

There is power in being the black sheep. It means you're different. It means you refuse to conform. It means your story was never supposed to look like theirs.

They spoke in doubt. I moved in faith.
They watched for me to fail. I rose higher.
They whispered. I worked. And now, they watch in silence.

So to every girl who's ever been called "too much," "not enough," or "a waste," I say this: Wear your crown. Shine anyway because the black sheep grows into the boldest lion.

Chapter 8
A Letter to My Son

My dearest *Rashawn*,

From the moment I knew I was carrying you, my life changed. I was only nineteen — still a girl in many ways — but I knew instantly that I had to become a woman for you. You didn't ask to be here, but you became my reason to live. My reason to fight. My reason to become.

I didn't grow up with the kind of love I wanted to give you. I was rejected, overlooked, and criticized — even by those who should've protected me. I never wanted you to feel that way. I made a promise to myself that you would know love. You would feel supported. You would feel wanted.

Raising you wasn't always easy. There were nights I cried myself to sleep because I didn't know how I'd get through the next day. I worked late shifts, stood on tired feet, and gave up sleep so you had what you needed. I worked right up until I gave birth to you. I did it gladly because you were worth it.

I made mistakes, son. I'm not perfect. But I've always tried to hide you from the storms I was walking through. I stayed strong even when I was breaking inside. You gave me a reason to keep pushing. And even when life knocked me down, your smile picked me back up.

You've grown into such a respectful, intelligent, and kind young man. And every time I look at you, I feel proud. Not just of who you are, but of how far we've come together.

If you take anything from my journey, let it be this:

- No matter what obstacles come your way, keep pushing.
- Never let anyone tell you who you are or what you're worth.
- Know that even when you feel alone, God is there — and so am I.
- And never forget: **You are loved. Deeply. Fiercely. Unconditionally.**

I may not have had a perfect past, but I fought hard to give you a better future. And I will keep fighting, praying, and showing up — as your mother, your protector, and your biggest fan — for as long as I live.

With all my love,
Mom

Chapter 9
A Message to My Mother

To my mother,

For years, I have borne the burden of your words, the lack of your love, and the pain of your rejection. I desperately longed to be your daughter in a way that would make you proud. I sought your approval, your affection, and your embrace when the world felt overwhelming.

But instead, I felt like a burden. A mistake. Something you had to put up with rather than cherish.

You didn't truly see me. You ignored the things that brought me joy, like dance, cheerleading, and Junkanoo. You judged my rebellion but never asked about my pain. You punished me, pushed me away, and made me feel like I didn't belong in the very home I came from.

You called me your mistake.

Those words haunt me to this day.

But here's the truth: I was never a mistake. I was a blessing — even if you couldn't see it. Even if you never said it. Even if you never believed it.

There were times I hated you for the way you treated me. Times I cried myself to sleep, wondering why I wasn't enough for you. I spent years chasing love in all the wrong places because the love I needed from you was missing. And yes, I blamed you for a lot.

But today, I release all of that.

Because I finally realize that you, too, were broken. Maybe you were carrying your pain. Perhaps you didn't know how to love the way I needed to be loved. Maybe your silence and your anger were just your unhealed wounds passing down through generations.

So today, I choose forgiveness.

I forgive you for what you didn't know.

I forgive you for the hurt.

I forgive you for not showing up the way I needed.

Because holding on to that pain only kept me tied to the past. And I'm ready to be free.

I want you to know that despite everything, I made it. The black sheep became the boss. The rejected child became the resilient woman. The one you thought would fail is still standing, stronger than ever.

And I still hope — in the quiet corners of my heart — that one day, you'll see me. That one day, you'll understand the love I've had to teach myself.

But even if you don't, I'll be okay.

Because I've made peace with the woman in the mirror.

With honesty and healing,

Your daughter, Rashanda.

Chapter 10
Beauty from the Burn

There's something sacred about hitting rock bottom — because it's there, in the ashes of everything you thought would save you, that you discover what you're made of.

I had been through fire: heartbreak, abandonment, abuse, addiction, betrayal, rejection, loneliness — you name it. I didn't just feel pain — I *lived* in it. I wore it. I woke up with it. And yet somehow, I still managed to get up.

They observed the outside: the barmaid, the single mother, the "troubled" girl who moved from one place to another, jumping between jobs, and remaining in a long, aimless relationship. However, they were unaware of the nights I silently prayed, crying on the bathroom floor. They didn't see me sleeping in a car while pregnant, pleading with God to help me survive just one more night.

And God indeed did so. Each and every time.

I used to wonder if He noticed me at all. Now, I realize He was with me all along. My salvation wasn't the usual churchy, perfect, religious type. I didn't wear long skirts or quote Scripture with ease. However, I truly believed— believed in a God who saw the real me and loved me regardless.

The broken girl.
The loud one.
The one who cursed, doubted, and fought back.
The one who stayed too long and left too late.

That girl was still worthy. Still chosen. Still covered.

Gradually, I began to rebuild—not from what was given to me, but from what I survived. I poured myself into my businesses. I created spaces where I didn't have to shrink, apologize, or prove myself. I made room for joy again. For purpose. For peace.

And what I learned is this:

- You don't come out of the fire the same.
- You don't survive hell and go back to pretending.
- You rise — scarred, but stunning.
- Burned, but bold.

There is beauty in the burn because the woman I am now? She's unstoppable. Not because life didn't try to break her, but because it *did*, and she's still standing.

Chapter 11
Letting Go to Grow

There comes a moment when holding on hurts more than letting go.

I held onto things that no longer served me—people, habits, environments, and beliefs. I stayed attached because it felt familiar, even when it was hurting me. I clung because I was afraid of the unknown. But what I didn't realize was that in holding on, I was also holding myself *back*.

I stayed in a loveless relationship for the sake of stability and security. I convinced myself that survival was more important than happiness. But deep down, I was shrinking. I was sacrificing peace for comfort and comfort for chaos.

Letting go didn't mean I hated anyone—it just meant I was finally choosing me.

I had to let go of:

- The need to be accepted by a family that never truly saw me.
- The idea that I needed a man to feel complete.
- The guilt of not being the version of "Rashanda" everyone expected.
- The trauma I never asked for but carried anyway.

Letting go was scary. It meant standing on my own two feet, fully. But I realized—I'd been doing that all along.

Every challenge had already prepared me. Every heartbreak had already stretched me. Every tear I cried watered the soil for my growth.

And as I started releasing those weights, I felt lighter. Freer. Clearer.

I began focusing on the things that fueled me—my boutique, my kitchen, and my dreams. I provided my son with not just a mother, but a role model of resilience. I stopped pursuing love and started embracing *wholeness*.

Growth doesn't come from holding on; it comes from letting go. Releasing what hurts, walking away from what limits you, and trusting that what's ahead is better than what's behind.

I am no longer the girl who relied on others to save her. Now, I am a woman who has saved herself by prioritizing peace over pressure, purpose over pain, and trusting God instead of succumbing to fear.

Chapter 12
From Ashes to Authority

If you had told my younger self—the broken girl with tear-stained cheeks and a heavy heart—that she would someday walk in authority, I don't think she would've believed you.

But here I am.

I rose from ashes—the kind that come from things burning to the ground. My childhood, my identity, my relationships, my sense of worth—all of it went through fire. I was stripped, shattered, and silenced. But I was never *done*.

What they meant to destroy me only prepared me for leadership.

What they meant to shame me only deepened my purpose.

What the enemy used to break me, God used to build me.

I now walk with my head high—not because everything is perfect, but because I've earned this posture. I've bled for it. Fought for it. I have prayed through it. I've looked in the mirror, faced my demons, and declared, *"Not anymore."*

I took charge of my destiny.
I broke generational patterns.
I raised a respectful, intelligent son.
I created a name for myself—a woman who defied every label placed on her.

No longer the black sheep.
No longer the victim.
No longer is the girl begging to be loved.

Now, I am a woman of vision. A woman of strength. A woman who doesn't just survive but leads, uplifts, and inspires.

The phrase **"from ashes to authority"** represents my truth. It's proof that God doesn't waste pain. That no tear was in vain. Everything I endured served a purpose.

And now, I speak to the next woman reading this who feels like she's still in the fire:

Your ashes are not the end.

- You will rise.
- You will lead.
- You will heal.
- And you, too, will walk in authority.

If I succeeded, *so can you.*